12 Steps t(
A Journal of
...to J

"I don't know anyone who wouldn't want to be mind-blowingly happy... I hope everyone takes advantage of this. I know everyone wants to be happy, and a lot of people just don't know how to do that. They never had that emotional education, and you're providing that for people."

—Jack Canfield, Co-Author of the Chicken Soup for the Soul™ series and a Pioneer in the Field of Personal Development and Peak Performance

"Trish encourages readers to challenge unfulfilling expectations, unhealthy emotional responses, incongruent spiritual practices and other behaviors that are blocking them from experiencing self-actualized lives. She provokes the reader to dig deep in exploring how these issues cause pain, restrict growth and result in patterns inconsistent with their desires. This is a must-read for anyone, but especially Black women who want to break free and take flight in the next chapter of their lives!"

—Regina S. Brown, PsyD, Licensed Psychologist

"This inspirational journal is a refreshing guide on how you can begin the journey of making meaningful changes in your life. We all just need a little courage to start the process. If you are looking to evolve to a happier and more juicy life, *12 Steps to Mind-Blowing Happiness* is for you!"

—Natasha Brewley (Chef Beee), MBA, PhD, HHC,
    Owner of Essentially Chef Beee and Nyansapo Wellness Institute, Inc.

"Trish Ahjel Roberts draws on her lived experiences with generosity and skill, presenting a 12-step approach to creating a more self-actualized (and joyful) life. *12 Steps to Mind-Blowing Happiness* offers something for all women everywhere looking to live a more authentic life."

—Julie Hartley, MFA, Director, Centauri Arts Writing School, Ontario, CN

"As much as I'm a huge advocate for social justice, I'm also a huge advocate for mental health. *12 Steps to Mind-Blowing Happiness* is an interactive journal that allows you to be open and honest with yourself and teaches you how to be the happiest and best version of yourself."

—Mona Swain, Theater Actress and TikTok Influencer

"Trish's book is a 12-step guide to an authentic and joyful life for anyone who is willing to put in the effort. So many self-help tomes neglect her first piece of advice: Heal the Past First. They encourage action towards the future without first addressing the past, which often anchors us in place. She weaves in wisdom from the Buddhist tradition that she and I share. For example, the chapters on anger and patience are teachings of Buddha on how to live a life of peace and love. I recommend this book to anyone looking to develop their own personal identity and path."

—Paul B. Chen, Publisher, Natural Awakenings – Atlanta

"This is a perfect journal for anyone beginning their journey of self-discovery or even in the thick of working to figure things out. Trish shows us how beautiful this process of growth and transformation can be when we listen to our inner calling and step bravely into who we're meant to be."

—Jaimee Ratliff, Owner, Yoga with Jaimee, LLC

"I am so inspired by *12 Steps to Mind-Blowing Happiness*. Following each powerful lesson, Trish gives journaling prompts to help you process the information and deep feelings that may have arisen. Finally, she makes it all light with quizzes at the end and a music playlist. I'm totally feeling this book!"
—Sonia Kidd, Coaching Client and Business Owner

"I loved that this book was quick and easy to read. Sometimes I'm too busy to start a long book and will put off reading because I won't have time to finish. The way this book is set up, there are blank pages after each chapter so you can jot down notes and answer questions. You have the option to read straight through or randomly. I read it first, then went back to the chapters I wanted to revisit. And, don't be fooled, although *12 Steps to Mind-Blowing Happiness* is a quick read, it packs a lifetime of helpful suggestions, affirmations and insights that will serve as a soothing and friendly guide on your journey to a happier life. There is something for everyone, and you will see yourself along the way."
—Melanie Murillo, Coaching Client and Government Employee

"I've had the opportunity to work with Trish as a coaching client. She provides such a lovely framework to search deeper into your heart's desires and passions, while giving you the courage to realize your authentic self. *12 Steps to Mind-Blowing Happiness* really inspired me and gently nudged me to think about the possibilities in my life in a different way. Trish provides the roadmap to start a beautiful journey, no matter where you are in your life."
—Tamara Guillou, Coaching Client and Corporate Executive

"So many of us are moving through our daily lives without stopping to consider if we could be doing more, giving more, being more. *12 Steps to Mind-Blowing Happiness* poses the questions many of us don't think to ask. Trish offers a fresh perspective that challenges us to open to new possibilities and become our best selves. Her words are so liberating and inspirational, she lit a fire inside of me! I can't wait to see where her 12-step process takes me."
—Lisa Martin Suber, Children's Book Author
  and Atlanta Public School Teacher

"*12 Steps to Mind Blowing Happiness* inspires readers to never settle for mediocrity, embrace change, and dream BIG! Enough of sitting around and hoping for good to come. This is the key to all of your locked doors."
—Kayla George, College Student

"*12 Steps to Mind-Blowing Happiness* is a must-read for anyone who is dissatisfied with her life, stuck in old habits or simply searching for a greater connection with self. Trish addresses difficult topics that most of us just hope will fade into the background and never return again, not realizing that if we don't come to terms with our past, we cannot create a fully abundant future. Trish guides us down this path with humor, humility, and compassion. I personally feel a greater connection with self and the world at large as a result of this beautiful journal."
—Cindy Parker, Administrative Director,
  Kadampa Meditation Center, Atlanta GA

Twelve Steps to Mind-Blowing Happiness

*A Journal of Insights, Quotes & Questions
to Juice Up Your Journey*

by Trish Ahjel Roberts

For permission or corrections:
Email: hello@trishahjelroberts.com

First Edition: November 2020
Second Edition: August 2021

Printed in the United States of America

Cover Design: Oliviaprodesign

Digital Art: Kayla T. George

Photo Credit: Perfectly Captured Photography

ISBN: 9781737595205

Access FREE self-care e-book at http://busywomanguide.com

Mind-Blowing Happiness (*noun*)

A state of deep joy and fulfillment characterized by a juicy life journey steeped in passion, purpose and the realization of your fullest potential.

"Happiness is like a butterfly; the more you chase it, the more it will elude you, but if you turn your attention to other things, it will come and sit softly on your shoulder."
–Henry David Thoreau

Thank you to Marci Shimoff, Jack Canfield, Patty Aubery, Steve Harrison,
Iyanla Vanzant, Mary Giuseffi, Alesha Peluso, Tamara Guillou
and everyone who has joined or supported me on this
journey of Healing, Spirituality, Connection, Authenticity,
Self-Love, Peace, Generosity, Detachment, Surrender,
Patience, Compassion, Passion and Freedom.
These are the steps to self-actualization
and mind-blowing happiness.

❧ ❧ ❧

"Yesterday I was clever, so I wanted to change the world.
Today I am wise, so I am changing myself."
–Rumi

I Am.

I know the essence of the fruit tree,
the dream of the ocean,
the song of the butterfly.

I have been mother of the orphan,
goddess of the universe,
lover of humanity and creator of time.

I will ignite the passion of the planet,
spread kindness like fire
and provide refuge for those in ashes.

I wear the crystals of the gods,
the malas of the spirit
and the carvings of the ancestors.

I see a world of symbiosis,
deeply intertwined community
and the love of Oshun and Athena.

I feel elevated,
supported by wings that soar toward the heavens
and span the width of the universe.

I have lived a million lives
as goddess and buddha,
man and woman,
farm animal and king.

I know the secret of limitless joy,
eternal bliss
and sublime surrender.

I share with those
who are seekers
of the most ultimate
and profound wisdom.

Trish Ahjel Roberts

Contents

FOREWORD

During this transformational time on the planet, we've been facing innumerable challenges including a worldwide pandemic, climate change, and political unrest. Amongst all of the strife in the world, it's quite an inspiring idea to think we can be... happy!

Trish Ahjel Roberts takes it one step further and says that we can have what she calls Mind-Blowing Happiness™. I wholeheartedly agree.

At this pivotal juncture in humanity, just surviving is no longer an option, as that only keeps us in states of fear and lack. Instead, we're here to learn how to thrive at our highest levels and experience the abundance of incredible happiness, joy, and fulfillment that's available to each of us.

By saying yes to Mind-Blowing Happiness™, you're making the choice to step out of a fear-based model of life and into a life of joy, passion, purpose and service.

I've been on a happiness journey throughout my life. I was born depressed and was on a decades-long quest to learn the true secrets to happiness. After interviewing hundreds of deeply happy people, I discovered that the main difference between happy people and others is simply that they have different habits. I started practicing those happiness habits myself and they worked so well that I couldn't wait to share them in my book, *Happy for No Reason.*

Trish has also had an incredible personal journey to greater happiness that inspired her to create *12 Steps to Mind-Blowing Happiness.*

She knows what it's like to experience trauma, abuse, great loss, and institutional racism. She's a living example that no matter how many challenges or setbacks you've experienced in life, Mind-Blowing Happiness™ is available to you.

As a sought-after life coach and an expert in both Buddhist and yogic philosophies, Trish has a unique ability to present difficult subjects with a sense of joyful determination for what's on the other side of the journey. She cheers you on with the confident, guiding voice of a woman who not only teaches, but lives her work.

Throughout the book, Trish shares insights, quotes and questions that will inspire and empower you to move toward your dreams with confidence. She also offers practical resources to support you along the way. Each of her brief essays awakens your inner wisdom while each question nudges you along your personal path to reach your richest and most beautiful life. All the while, she adds an endearing playfulness with her approach as she encourages you to "juice up your journey."

12 Steps to Mind-Blowing Happiness is a powerful tool for creating a joyful, fulfilling, passion-filled life. With the help of this beautiful journal, may you find your own unique path to Mind-Blowing Happiness™!

–Marci Shimoff, #1 *New York Times* Bestselling Author of *Happy for No Reason* and *Chicken Soup for the Woman's Soul*, and Featured Teacher in *The Secret*

WELCOME TO THE 2ND EDITION!

I wrote the first version of *12 Steps to Mind-Blowing Happiness* at the end of 2020. The world was grappling with the reality of a global pandemic that had taken over 500,000 lives in the United States alone. We were processing not only our sense of isolation but our core values. *Who are we when nobody is around to judge or validate us?*

Our Declaration of Independence states that "All (people) are created equal, that they are endowed by their Creator with certain unalienable Rights, that among these are Life, Liberty and the pursuit of Happiness." And yet, many of us have become disconnected from both our sense of happiness and our own spirituality. We may question our purpose and wonder if we even deserve a life of passion and joy.

I'm here to tell you that not only do you *deserve* the best life has to offer, but it is also *possible* to improve all areas of your life with a little time and attention. In other words, Mind-Blowing Happiness™ is attainable.

My journey to the idea of Mind-Blowing Happiness™ began when I studied Maslow's needs hierarchy when I was in business school. Abraham Maslow was an American psychologist who is best known for creating a theory of psychological health based on fulfilling human needs in priority, culminating with self-actualization. While the needs don't fall into perfect order, I'm sure you will see the logic. First, you must take care of your basic needs for food, shelter and safety before you move on to more complex goals like intimacy, self-esteem and respect. It is a helpful tool for assessing our journey through life. Here's a graphic representation:

Maslow's Hierarchy of Needs

SELF-ACTUALIZATION:
Full Potential

ESTEEM:
Confidence, Respect, Achievement

LOVE AND BELONGING:
Friendship, Intimacy, Family, Connection

SAFETY:
Personal Security, Employment, Resources, Health

BASIC:
Food, Water, Shelter, Clothing, Rest

While Maslow pointed out the needs, he did not provide a path to attain them. Through many years of studying Buddhist and yogic philosophies, life coaching strategies and therapeutic techniques, and my personal experiences overcoming trauma in many forms, the *12 Steps to Mind-Blowing Happiness* materialized in my life. It is my pleasure to share these teachings with you so that you can experience the deepest levels of joy and fulfillment in your own life. This mission is so important to me that I've made the commitment to teach the *12 Steps to Mind-Blowing Happiness* to 12 million people over the next 12 years.

Mind-Blowing Happiness™ is a state of deep joy and fulfillment characterized by a juicy life journey steeped in passion, purpose and the realization of your fullest potential. The world needs not only this sense of joy but the dedication to service that arises from it. When you rise to your potential, the whole world will benefit. Take a moment to imagine a self-actualized world. Now that you know where we're going, get ready for the ride. Trust me. It's juicy!

–Trish Ahjel Roberts

Why Mind-Blowing?

Everyone wants happiness and freedom from suffering. You, me, animals and even insects. If you don't think insects want to be happy, all you have to do is try killing one. They will fight to the end for their lives just like you or me. The desire for mind-blowing happiness, however, is unique to humans. We are able to access our Divine consciousness in ways that other species simply cannot. This innate ability gives rise to a profound desire for exceptional joy, purpose and fulfillment.

This journal is carefully designed to walk you through the 12-drop approach presented in the self-help memoir, *Thinking Outside the Chrysalis: A Black Woman's Guide to Spreading Her Wings*, and can be used alone or in conjunction with that book. This approach was developed over years of studying Buddhist and yogic philosophies, life coaching strategies and therapeutic techniques. I share the wisdom I've learned while providing the space for you to craft your own story and alter the trajectory of your life. I often speak of the Universe and Divinity. You might prefer the word God. Understand these words refer to the same energy that some may call the "I Am." These all reference an organized higher power. You may substitute my words for whatever feels most comfortable to you.

Begin with the Mind-Blowing Happiness Assessment Quiz on page 153. As you progress through the chapters, meditate on the quotes, read the insights, and answer the questions with an open heart. I offer two examples for each question in case you need help getting started. In most cases, your answers will be much longer and more complete. When you answer the questions, write freely. Try not to edit yourself. You will be surprised to see what bubbles to the surface. Don't worry if you find yourself writing more than what was asked of you. More is better. Write freely on anything the topic unearths for you. We all have inherent wisdom within us. Journaling with the guidance of prompts allows that knowledge to come to the forefront. The fifth question in each Step is an opportunity for visualization. Don't hold back. Engage all five senses as you imagine what your new reality feels like. How does it smell, taste, sound, look and feel? Include what I call the sixth sense, your gut reaction or intuition. According to Dr. Joe Dispenza in his work, *Tuning in to New Potentials*, visualization creates magnetic energy that brings our desires to us, so make sure to dig in deep.

Take time to enjoy the 12-track playlist and recorded meditations and affirmations related to each Step at TrishAhjelRoberts.com/resources. The last section, Organic Synergy, brings together all the energy from the Steps with additional exercises and assessments. At the end of the book, there is a list of resources to support you.

As you unfold the joyful truth in each Step, you will undoubtedly "juice up" your life's journey. When life is juicy it's rich, ripe and bubbling over. You realize there is so much inside of you. It's more than you knew and more than enough. Your cup overflows with abundance. You have so much goodness to share. You no longer worry about the things you used to. You are confident about the future. You wake up each day with joy and gratitude.

That's mind-blowing happiness. Now, let's get started.

Step 1: Unpack Your Bags
(Heal the Past First)

"If you're silent about your pain,
they'll kill you and say you enjoyed it."
–Zora Neale Hurston

It is impossible to live the life of your dreams with an unhealed heart. Journaling is a powerful healing practice. When combined with other modalities, whether formal or casual, it allows us to unpack our past hurts so we can fully experience our present with a new understanding and lightness.

Usually we know what has hurt us in the past, but sometimes it's not so clear. If we are survivors of violence or sexual assault it's unmistakable. If our pain is less obvious, it may be harder to define. Emotional abuse, bullying, race-based trauma, alcohol or drug-addicted parents, mental or physical ailments, dysfunctional family dynamics, sexism, homophobia or transphobia, and other forms of injury can manifest negatively in our lives. We can become withdrawn, insecure, anxious or dependent on a wide variety of bad habits or substances to make us feel better.

In his brilliant book, *My Grandmother's Hands: Racialized Trauma and the Pathway to Mending Our Hearts and Bodies*, Resmaa Menakem says, "Healing involves discomfort, but so does refusing to heal. And, over time, refusing to heal is always more painful." Some questions may be difficult. Remember you control your journey. If a response immediately rises to the surface, let it flow. If you find yourself at a loss for words, you may want to take time to ponder the question and return to it later. Come back in a few hours or even a few days.

As a self-actualization coach, I often talk about the Eight Main Life Areas. (There is a detailed explanation of these areas in the resource section at the back of this book.)

- Mental health and personal development
- Relationships
- Physical health
- Spiritual life
- Occupation
- Fun and recreation
- Money
- Physical environment (home/work)

Think about these areas as you work through the *12 Steps to Mind-Blowing Happiness*. When you are at your best, all of the life areas will be in harmony. For most of us, this takes time.

As you deepen your healing journey, you may want to work with a professional therapist, a therapeutic book, a support group, healing films and music, art or animal therapy, or some combination. Unpack your bags and heal yourself.

"If you don't have a test, you won't be able to have a testimony."
—Iyanla Vanzant

Describe your journey to healing. Have you started? Is it necessary? What is your first memory as a child? What memories are painful? What areas need work?

Example 1: I started my journey as a teenager when I got counseling for the first time and read a book about recovering from my parents' divorce...

Example 2: I haven't started a journey to healing. My first memory as a child is my mother reading to me. My painful memory is being teased in school. I never thought about healing from being teased, but I think that childhood teasing still affects how I feel about myself, so I think I may want to work on that...

What does wholeness mean to you? Describe a time when you felt completely whole and healed.

Use the Eight Main Life Areas (mental health and personal development, relationships, physical health, spiritual life, occupation, fun and recreation, money, physical environment) as a reference.

Example 1: For me, wholeness means all of the eight main life areas are in order. I'm feeling basically happy, and I'm not worried about money or relationships. I can sleep at night without feeling stressed out. I feel pretty whole and healed now...

Example 2: I felt completely whole and healed when I was ten years old, before I realized my mom was an alcoholic and before I experienced any trauma...

How was mental health handled in your family and community? How did that impact you?

Example 1: Mental health was never discussed in my family even though I had relatives who I later learned had mental health diagnoses. It left me unprepared to deal with my own bouts with anxiety and depression...

Example 2: My parents used to sit us down and talk to us about mental health. I think that made me more aware when dealing with my own issues or with people around me...

What steps do you need to take on your path to healing, recovery or wholeness?

Example 1: I think working through this journal and checking out some of the resources will help me on my path to healing. I will also consider working with a therapist...

Example 2: I've been in therapy for years and I feel really healed. As far as feeling whole and working with the Eight Main Life Areas, I really want to work on my financial situation and finding a better apartment to live in...

Visualize life when you are healed and whole in a consistent and permanent way. Describe your job, friends, family and recreation. Use all of your five senses and your sixth sense, your gut.

Example 1: I imagine sleeping well without financial worries and having lots of good friends. I work as a teacher and I travel internationally for fun. It smells like my mom's garden and feels like sun on my skin...

Example 2: I imagine laughing a lot and having time to exercise with my partner. I work as a researcher and I grow vegetables in my own garden. It smells like fresh mint and morning dew...

Step 2: Tap into Your Spirituality
(Get a Spiritual Life)

"Believe in nothing, no matter where you read it, or who said it,
no matter if I have said it, unless it agrees with your own
reason and your own common sense."
–Buddha

You cannot experience deep happiness and fulfillment without recognizing you are a spiritual being. This is not the same as being religious, although you can certainly be both. Spirituality is the recognition of the Divine spiritual consciousness in each of us. Christians often refer to this as the "holy ghost" or "holy spirit." Buddhists might refer to this as the "mental continuum" or "Buddha seed." In yoga, which is not a religion, we refer to this as the "Self." Note the capital "S." This spiritual energy resides in each of us, even if we are not familiar with it. Much like a diamond buried deep in the earth, we may not have found it. We may not even know it exists.

Whatever you were taught as a child or have come to believe, you are missing out if you do not recognize your own Divine spiritual self. Even if a particular religious tradition did not work for you, you are still a spiritual person. No matter whether you believe in heaven, hell, reincarnation or eternal slumber, it's hard to deny that inside this shell of a body there is a fire—a light, a soul, a spirit, a mental continuum. That little light of yours needs nurturing, and it is not your physical body. If you are not familiar with that inner spark, it's time to start the expedition. You will not find this precious jewel if you're not even looking.

For most people, questions concerning spirituality are easier than those related to healing. Just remember, you control your journey. Take as much time as you need to respond, and write until you have nothing left to say. As you progress on your spiritual journey, you may want to read or listen to spiritual books, watch films or join groups. Always bring your critical mind and question any teaching you encounter; unfortunately, there are con artists using religion to take advantage of people. I list some reputable resources at the end of this book. Your spiritual "Self" is waiting. Go ahead and give it a tap.

"There is a candle in your heart, ready to be kindled.
There is a void in your soul, ready to be filled."
—Rumi

Describe your spiritual journey. Have you started?

This might include your religious practices or other spiritual activities like meditation, yoga or prayer.

Example 1: I think my spiritual journey started when my sister died. That was the first time I really thought about what happens after you die. I was raised Christian so I started paying attention to my local church...

Example 2: I don't think I'm on a spiritual journey. I never thought about it before. I've taken a couple of yoga classes at the gym and I pray sometimes...

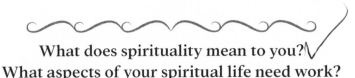

What does spirituality mean to you?
What aspects of your spiritual life need work?

Example 1: Spirituality is important to me. It's a part of everything I do. I would like to set aside more time for prayer and reading my bible...

Example 2: Spirituality is confusing for me. I belong to a church, but I've always thought of my religion as a way to worship God. I never thought of it as inner work. I'd like to learn more about working on my inner spiritual self...

How was religion and spirituality handled in your family and community? How do you feel your religious upbringing (or lack thereof) affected you?

Example 1: I grew up in a very religious family that made me feel ashamed. We went to church every Sunday which was nice because it was consistent, at least…

Example 2: I grew up without any kind of religion so I always felt left out when my friends celebrated religious holidays. My mom used to pray sometimes and I guess that counts as spiritual. I'm not sure how it's impacted me…

What steps do you need to take on
your path to spiritual fulfillment?

Example 1: I think I want to start reading spiritual books. My best friend is Muslim so maybe I will start with the Koran. I want to figure out what I believe for myself...

Example 2: I want to get back into bible study and find a regular church home. I'd also like to learn how to meditate...

Describe how you will look, feel, and act when you are at the height of spiritual awareness and joy. Include all five senses and your sixth sense.

Example 1: Wow. I guess at the height of spiritual awareness I will have a deep feeling of self-love. I will know I am a child of God. It will smell like strawberries! Lol! My skin will feel soft. It will sound like classical music! My stomach will be relaxed...

Example 2: I can't imagine this but I'll try. I guess I'll have a feeling about my inner Self that was discussed at the beginning of the chapter. Like, I'll feel that god is inside of me. Must smell and taste like chocolate. My belly will feel round. I won't be stressed out...

Step 3: Create Your Village
(It Takes a Village to Support an Adult)

> "If you want to go quickly, go alone.
> If you want to go far, go together."
> –African Proverb

You cannot attain a profoundly joyful life if you are isolated. Humans are deeply social creatures. When we are disconnected from other people we wither and dry up. Whether you consider yourself an introvert, extrovert or somewhere in between, we all need connection.

Western society is structured in a way that makes many of us feel lonely. We have individual goals and often live alone. Media and advertising encourage us to compete with our neighbors and keep up with the Joneses. Social media has us even more transfixed. We compare our homes, work, clothes, cars and relationships. Stepping away from this individuality and competition and leaning into community, collaboration and cooperation are critical to expanding our joy and fulfillment.

Reference the Eight Main Life Areas as you work through this Step. (A more detailed explanation is accessible on pg. 161.) You will want to create an authentic village in each area to provide the support you need for a juicy journey. Questions related to connection can be difficult depending on your circumstances. Take the time you need. As you build your village of support, it is critical that you give at least as much support as you receive. It is also extremely important that you surround yourself with positive people who are interested in personal development. The United States has reached a point where many people are being deceived by conspiracy theories, recruited by hate groups and incited by media and religious personalities. Seek communities based in love and you cannot fail. That means you must avoid racism, sexism, xenophobia, homophobia, transphobia, firearms and speciesism in the groups you join. Avoid hate and violence in all its forms. Even if these are areas you are still working on for yourself, it is helpful to join groups with people who are farther along the path toward uplifting and embracing others, non-harming, personal development and joy.

Some people you will pay to be in your village, like your doctor, therapist or personal trainer. Even in these relationships, you can show up with an extra smile, kind word, small gift or note of appreciation. Some relationships don't have an exchange of money, like family, friends, workout buddies and co-workers. These relationships have a powerful exchange of energy, which is even more important to notice. I list some of my favorite resources for connection at the end of this book. Your village is waiting, but you need to build it yourself. Let's get started.

"I alone cannot change the world, but I can cast
a stone across the waters to create many ripples."
—Mother Teresa

Describe your current support network. Describe the energy you feel from important people in your life.

Use the Eight Main Life Areas (mental health and personal development, relationships, physical health, spiritual life, occupation, fun and recreation, money, physical environment) as a reference.

Example 1: My support network consists of my husband, my mom, Reverend Liza, my therapist, Kate and Dr. Howser. I guess this book is my personal development support. I don't think I have work or financial support. Hubby takes care of the house, though. I don't think I get the best energy from Dr. Howser but everyone else makes me feel really supported...

Example 2: I don't have family support right now. It's mainly my best friend and my coach that I lean on. I've never had real mental health support except for my friends. My dad helps with the house and I love my teammates. Oh, and my boss is really great too...

What does community and connection mean to you? How would you describe the level of support you receive among family, friends and community? How would you describe the level of support you give to others?

Example 1: I've always felt pretty isolated. Mom has always had issues and I don't know where my dad is. I have a couple of decent friends, but I think I probably need to figure out how to get more support. I don't really give a lot of support except to my friends...

Example 2: I'm very active with the neighborhood block association, my church and my school. I feel pretty well supported and I think I give support back. I think I could probably still do better...

What did you learn growing up about what it means to support each other as a family? What did you learn as a child about community support?

Example 1: Growing up I was always responsible for the younger kids, so that was support in my family. Me doing everything! Lol! I don't know who was supposed to be supporting me though...

Example 2: Growing up it was just me and my grandmother. All we had was each other and the church. Now that granny's not here anymore, I don't know how to feel. I guess I learned that support comes from home and church...

What steps do you need to take to build a strong and authentic support network? Who or what do you need to let go of?

Example 1: I would like to reconnect with some of my old friends from school. I will start by looking them up on Facebook and LinkedIn. I also want to find a book club to meet on a monthly basis. I'll look at my community center and on meetup.com. I really need to let go of my babysitter...

Example 2: I need a new doctor. I don't feel like Dr. Clover listens to me. I'll go on zocdoc.com and on my healthcare website to find other options. I also want to join a gym to work out and meet some new people. I will Google local fitness centers and call to schedule a trial workout...

Describe how you will look, feel and act when you have the supportive "village" you imagine for yourself. Use all six senses. Imagine there is no one in your network who makes you feel unloved, stressed or unhappy.

Example 1: If I had a supportive village I wouldn't feel so isolated. I'd feel really safe and comfortable. It feels like a warm campfire, smells like wood burning, sounds like that crackle...

Example 2: I can't imagine not having people stressing me out. My own mother makes me crazy. I suppose I can learn to limit our interactions and focus more on building a positive community. Wow. That feels like sunshine and smells like daffodils. It makes my stomach feel really soft and relaxed...

Step 4: Love the Real You
(Get REAL with Someone)

"To be authentic is the highest form of praise.
You're fulfilling your mission and purpose on
earth when you honor the real you."
–Oprah Winfrey

If you want to be happy, you have to learn to love yourself in a meaningful way. We are not born knowing ourselves, let alone loving ourselves. We have an instinct for physical survival, so we will protect our bodies in most scenarios. We do not have that same instinct for our minds. It must be developed. Trying to cultivate self-love without self-awareness is like slicing bread before it's baked. The New Oxford dictionary defines self-awareness as "conscious knowledge of one's own character, feelings, motives and desires." This Step encourages us to learn about ourselves so we can love ourselves wholeheartedly. It also helps us grow desired qualities while reprogramming false messages from others, whether they are our families, friends or the media. When we love ourselves, we protect our bodies, minds and hearts. We establish boundaries against mental, spiritual and emotional abuse. We do not pretend to be anything we are not. We are not scared to speak our mind with kindness and love. We take responsibility for our shortcomings.

We work to improve ourselves. We know we are imperfect but are grateful for our progress.

There are times when we cannot say, do or wear whatever we want. When we are required or decide to wear "masks" or uniforms, we should do so with awareness. These might be physical like makeup, hair, nails or a business suit. They may be subtle like emotional walls, or profound like holding on to secrets nobody else knows. If you want to be authentic, you must come to terms with your masks and uniforms. Know what you're hiding behind or adorning and why. That self-awareness is the path to authenticity and self-love.

Our beauty is in our quirky and unique flaws and imperfections. It's in our ability to delight in our physical features unapologetically. We cannot be genuinely happy if we can't be ourselves inside and out. There is no more striking combination than authenticity and confidence. Your identity and self-worth arise from your humanity and your Divine consciousness, not your role or outward appearance. The process of self-reflection and unearthing can be awkward, but the reward is so deep and juicy it's worth the effort. You won't be unsure of who you are and what you believe in, you will know.

From this place of authenticity, deeper friendships will arise. You may notice unhealthy relationships begin to fall away. Don't chase them. New friends who appreciate the confident, authentic YOU will find you exactly where you are.

For additional support on the topic of Deepening Self-Love, turn to page 163.

"After years of searching, I have found my soulmate, and it is myself."
—*Marci Shimoff*

Have you tried enough activities, groups or areas of interest to have a good sense of what you do and don't like? Describe at least twenty things you want to experience before you die.

Example 1: I've had lots of experiences: riding a motorcycle, traveling with the military and going skydiving. I think I have a good sense of what I like. Before I die, I want to get married, have a baby, own a business, have a garden, own my home, run a 5k...

Example 2: My mother has always worried so much about me, I think I've been scared to try a lot of things. I think I need to explore more to figure out what I really like, as opposed to what is just my family's traditions. Before I die, I want to have amazing sex, go to Hawaii, fall in love, buy a new car...

What types of "masks" and uniforms do you wear and why? How would you describe your journey toward loving your true self? Have you started? What areas still need work?

Example 1: I like to wear acrylic nails and a full face of makeup. I don't feel pretty unless my makeup, hair and nails are done. For work, I just wear my nurse's uniform. On weekends I like to dress and feel sexy. I think I'm just starting to think about who I really am...

Example 2: I wear makeup, a business suit and straighten my hair for work. On the weekends, I just put my hair in a ponytail and wear leggings. I've been working on myself for a few years now. First in my walk with God and then with some other self-help books and meditation. I still need to figure out my passion...

Was self-awareness, authenticity or self-love discussed in your family or community? How did that impact you?

Example 1: My parents taught me to tell the truth. I suppose that's authenticity. Although my mom loved to dress up and wear makeup. Honestly, I don't think my parents were very self-aware at all. They pretty much followed the church leaders. I think that's why I've never thought much about my own thoughts or desires more than superficially...

Example 2: My mom and dad were true hippies. I grew up watching them do Buddhist meditations and kundalini yoga. I always wanted to be different from them, so I never showed any interest in what they were doing. I think that kept me from exploring those types of things...

Name at least fifty things you love about yourself.

Internal or external. Be specific. If you have trouble, identify people you admire and name qualities they have that you want to develop.

Example 1: I think I love a lot of things about myself. 1. I'm kind. 2. I'm tall 3. I've got a nice boyfriend 4. I'm funny. 5. I've got curly hair. 6. I've got long legs. 7. I'm a good artist 8. I'm a great cook...

Example 2: I have a hard time thinking about things I love. I really admire Oprah Winfrey and Beyonce. I want to be 1. Confident, 2. Rich, 3. Smart, 4. Educated, 5. Self-employed, 6. in a great relationship, 7. More kind...

Describe what the world will look like when you are at the height of self-awareness, authenticity, and self-love. Where do you live? Who are your friends? How do you feel? Explore all six senses.

Example 1: The height of self-love? Welp, I guess I'll be living in a mansion in the French countryside. Well, maybe the USA countryside. I'll have my same close friends. I think I'll be really relaxed. It will look like sunshine and smell like cut grass. I'll feel warm...

Example 2: I really wish I could feel that comfortable being myself. If I could get there I think I would sleep better. I'd feel cool and calm. My stomach would relax. It will smell like oranges and look like gentle rain...

Step 5: Release the Anger Option
(Anger is a Lie)

"Exaggeration is truth that has lost its temper."
–Kahlil Gibran

It is impossible to be angry and happy simultaneously. One sucks the air out of a room while the other fills it with light. Imagine walking into a place where everyone is angry. Would you feel safe? Now imagine walking into a space where everyone is happy. Can you feel the difference?

One of my favorite and most misunderstood topics is anger. There is no situation when anger is helpful. Outrage is a natural response to injustice, insult or injury, but it does not have to graduate to anger. When we allow anger to take root, we lose our perspective. We are no longer able to make smart, calculated decisions. We find ourselves moving at the speed of our anger, rising to violence, threat or intimidation. We try to hurt others the way we have been hurt. We can no longer see people and things as they really are, but rather through the distorted lens of our wrath. Instead, take a few deep breaths and make some space for clarity. Practice patience and develop your compassion. (These will come up again in Steps #9 and #10.) Learn to meditate. Visit TrishAhjelRoberts.com/resources to access a variety of guided meditations.

The day I learned anger is unnecessary was the day I moved toward freedom. Both the Buddhist and Christian faiths warn about the perils of anger. In yogic philosophy, "Ahimsa," or non-harming is the first lesson. Anger always harms. That is its nature. If it doesn't drive you to harm others, it slowly eats away at you causing you to harm yourself. Many stress-related diseases are fed by anger. You don't have to go that route. Anger is a choice.

It takes some work but releasing the anger option is more than worth the effort. Anger allows us to feel falsely empowered while hiding from our pain. It delays solutions to our problems. It tricks us into believing it is a reliable friend. So how do we reduce our anger? The first step is to stop believing in it. It is never helpful.

Anger is the outgrowth of the pain you feel when things don't happen as you think they should. It's a tumor that needs to be removed. This does not mean you repress your anger or ignore your emotions. It means you open the door to work through your real emotions, usually an extremely busy ego coupled with pain. It means you reframe your anger, looking at the bigger picture with compassion and patience.

There is no way to experience mind-blowing happiness if you are frequently angry. You will be like a butterfly trying to fly with a hornet on its back. Anger cannot elevate you. It will buzz in your ear, throw you off course, and weigh you down.

The anger response will not disappear overnight, but once you accept the fact that anger serves absolutely no purpose, you can begin to release the anger option. Once you do, get ready to have your mind blown!

"Without inner peace outer peace is impossible."
—Geshe Kelsang Gyatso

Describe your relationship with anger.
How frequently do you feel angry, including more subtle versions of anger, like disappointment, frustration or annoyance? How does your anger affect you physically and mentally?

Example 1: I don't think of myself as an angry person, but I think I get annoyed and frustrated every day. As far as my relationship with anger, I think it's the same as everyone that I know. When I get angry, I feel sick to my stomach...

Example 2: I think I mostly go with the flow. I don't get impatient or annoyed very often, although I think I can do better with my kids. When I get angry, I feel my hair stand on end and sometimes I get a headache or I cry...

What does peacefulness mean to you?
What times in your life have you felt most at peace?
What times during your day are you most peaceful?

Example 1: Sometimes I think peacefulness sounds boring.
I think I like drama. I can't remember ever feeling at peace,
but I think I'm most peaceful at bedtime or first thing in the
morning...

Example 2: Being at peace is important to me. I felt most at
peace as a child when I didn't have to make a living. I usually
take a walk at lunchtime. That's when I feel most peaceful...

How was anger managed in your family in your youth?
How did that affect you?

Example 1: My father was always angry growing up and my mom never challenged him. I think that made me feel like I shouldn't express my real emotions. When dad was angry everyone in the house got quiet...

Example 2: I grew up in a peaceful household. My parents seem to get along. We never talked about anger or resolving conflict. I think we were just expected to be kind and diplomatic...

What steps would you need to take to remove anger from your life? Prioritize your list. What needs to happen first, second, etc.?

Example 1: I think I would have to learn to think about the things that normally make me angry in a different way. I need tools to help me stop getting angry. I think first I'd have to really convince myself I don't need to be angry. After that, I think I want to learn to meditate and lean more on my spiritual life...

Example 2: I think I need to end relationships that are upsetting. I really need to break up with my boyfriend. He's been verbally abusive for years now. I may even need to stop talking to my mom. She belittles me all the time...

**Imagine how you will feel living a life free from anger.
Take a few minutes to visualize this life. How do you
interact with your co-workers, family and friends?
How do you feel about yourself? Where do you live?
Who surrounds you? How's your health?
Use all six senses.**

Example 1: At first I thought it would be boring, but I think a life without anger could be nice. I could still be passionate about things that make me happy. I would smile a lot with my family and friends. I'd live someplace peaceful like on a farm or a beach. I'd be surrounded by water. My health would be amazing. It would sound like water and smell like dirt. The air would be moist...

Example 2: I don't know how I would feel without anger. I think I would miss it. I don't know why. I still think I would feel really good about myself. Maybe I'd finally be able to move into the city. It would smell like bus fumes and ivy. I would actually be really happy with that...

Step 6: Throw the Boomerang
(Give it Away for Free)

"If you only have one smile in you,
give it to the people you love."
–Maya Angelou

There is no such thing as a happy miser. As a matter of fact, "miser" is part of the word, "miserable." That's not a mistake. The Latin word "miser" actually means "miserable." Do you see where I'm going with this? In order to be happy, you must be generous.

If you want to grow, produce, explode or find any form of mind-blowing happiness, first you must share your gifts with the world. Don't worry if you don't know what your gifts are yet. We all have them. As you work toward self-awareness they will rise to the surface. Everyone is talented. You may not be a singer or an athlete, you might keep a well-organized home, cook amazing meals or work well with children. You might be a wonderful caregiver or encourager. Perhaps you have a mind for math or art. Whatever your talents, you must make the decision to share them. If we are not here to share our gifts, what are we here for? It cannot be to work hard for someone else's dream, hoard cash and die without identifying, honing or sharing our natural abilities. Identifying your talents and sharing them will renew your sense of vitality, joy and freedom. Those are ingredients for happiness of the mind-blowing variety.

When we share our time, talents and resources with the world, it comes back to us every single time. Western societies often teach the opposite. We should be paid for our efforts. Wealth is most important. We glorify the misery of the grind. Someone sold us on the narrative that if we work ourselves into exhaustion, cognitive dissonance, poor health and moral dilemmas, we will achieve Nirvana. Often our culture teaches us that we have to "look out for number one." This creates a miserly mindset. And, that can only lead to misery.

Open your heart and release your talents into the world. Let them shine in the light of day for all to see. Be fearless. The Universe will smile on you and respond with blessings that will surprise you, just like a boomerang.

"It is in giving that we receive."
—St. Francis of Assisi

Name the times in the last year that you did for others without expecting anything in return. What were those experiences like?

Example 1: I often hold doors open for people and I donate at the grocery store. I babysit my neighbor's dog when they travel. I pay my tithes. It makes me feel good, but I do get upset when people don't say thank you...

Example 2: When I do things for other people I expect something in return. If I serve on a charity, I expect to make good contacts for my business. I watch my grandchildren for free. I guess that is only for love and it feels better than the charity work...

What does generosity mean to you?
What times in your life have you felt most generous?
Think back to your childhood and into the present.

Example 1: For me, generosity means you get taken advantage of a lot. It means you're a giver and lots of people are ready to take. I don't remember feeling really generous in my life. I think my mom taught me early on to take what I can get...

Example 2: To me generosity is biblical. Jesus was always helping people, so I try to follow his lead. I felt most generous when I joined my church leadership. When I think back to childhood, I remember always being good about sharing my toys...

Did you grow up in a family that gave their time, talents, money or other resources freely? How did this affect you and your family? Who are your models for generosity?

Example 1: I grew up poor and my family didn't have much to give. Even with that, we always had an uncle or an aunt staying with us. I guess they were worse off than we were. It made me realize that family always comes first. My mom was my model...

Example 2: Mom and Dad always complained about paying taxes and supporting people who didn't want to work. I think they cheated people in their businesses. But they always gave to our school. I think they only gave when there was something in it for them...

What steps do you need to take to identify your talents?
How can you be more giving with your own resources of talent, time and money?

If you're not sure where to start, ask family and friends what you're best at. Also take notes of the times during the day when you find yourself smiling or deeply engrossed in your work/activity.

Example 1: I know I'm a good athlete and dancer. I get along with most people really well. My family thinks I'm good at being organized and on schedule. I think I could do more to coach young athletes and dancers...

Example 2: I've never thought about my talents before. I know I'm good at my job as a paramedic. I need to discuss with my family and friends. I think it would also be good if I tried some new classes at the community center to see what I like. Once I figure out what I'm good at, I guess I need to find some way to share it...

Take a few moments to imagine how you will feel living a life where you freely share your unique talents with others. Inhale all of it: the weather, your clothes, the aroma of food cooking. Immerse yourself in a vision of a wildly generous and free life. Don't forget to examine your gut feeling, that sixth sense.

Example 1: I'm going to imagine that I have a really special talent for teaching, and I teach children something that really changes who they grow up to be. They become really kind, generous people. And I paint pictures for all the kids to give then when they graduate from high school so my whole community can see my paintings. It makes me feel happy. I see blue skies. My clothes are really comfortable. I smell smores on the firepit. My gut is relaxed...

Example 2: I know I'm really good at making TikTok videos and iMovies. I imagine making videos for nonprofits for free so that all the charities I care about can attract more donors. I would start with the nursing home where my grandma is. The staff would be so happy. That makes me feel good. I see sunshine in a forest. I smell the forest moss...

Step 7: Learn to Detach
(No More Bag Lady)

"I freed a thousand slaves. I could have freed a thousand
more if only they knew they were slaves."
–Harriet Tubman

If we want to be genuinely happy, we must loosen our mental and physical grip on people, things and situations. We cannot be happy if we are clinging to everyone and everything in fear. Imagine loving someone so much you squeeze them until they suffocate, or at least, run away. Imagine racing into a burning building to save a treasured family heirloom and losing your life in the process. These are examples of attachment gone awry. We need to learn to detach. When we are happy and fulfilled, we don't feel the same need to hang on to people and things out of fear. We hold our loved ones and our favorite things lightly, with joy and hope, not worry and anxiety.

Everything around us, including people, are temporary. In time we will be separated by all types of changes, including illness and death. Children change every day and will eventually become adults. Young adults will become old. It can seem like a harsh reality, but we cause ourselves and others more pain when we get too attached to how things used to be. Once we accept the realities of change and impermanence, we can cherish our loved ones better knowing one day they won't be with us. And, if they are with us, it won't be in the same way. This helps us to spend our time wisely, preparing for the inevitability of change. Detachment helps us recognize the value of every moment, stay present and develop flexibility. It does not mean we love our family or the world any less, it actually lets us love more.

We all instinctively desire freedom. Slavery or servitude is the ultimate nightmare. Yet through our fear, we grip the people, traditions and possessions in our lives so tightly that we create pain for ourselves and our loved ones. We may find ourselves in codependent relationships, putting our own needs last while creating unhealthy fixations with our partner's issues.

Attachment is the same, whether we cling to our memories or physical items from the past. We hold onto things that weigh us down, while people in need go without. Donate, recycle, discard and create space, both mental and physical.

When we let go of attachment to safety and certainty, we can have our first glimpse of mental freedom. When we remove clutter from our home or workspace, it creates a physical freedom. By relinquishing both mental and physical burdens, we can learn to soar. It will take some effort, but this lightness is a main ingredient in mind-blowing happiness. Create space in your heart and home so profound joy and fulfillment can move in.

"Detachment is not that you should own nothing.
But that nothing should own you."
—Ali ibn abi Talib

Name five people or things you worry about losing. How do you think your worry impacts you? How does it impact other people? What do you think about hoarding vs. minimalism and sentimentalism vs. bucking tradition?

Example 1: I worry about everybody. I'm terrified something will happen to one of the kids or my husband. I think it drives them crazy. The only things I worry about are things with sentimental value. My granny's china, her throw pillows and my ring from grandpa. I had to google minimalism. It seems extreme to me, like hoarding. I like my stuff and I'm definitely sentimental. It's hard to think about not being attached...

Example 2: I think I'm more of a minimalist. I don't like a lot of clutter and I like simple things. I try to give away a lot of stuff. I am totally attached to my family. I can't imagine us not being together, although I know it's true one day we won't be together. I do worry a lot about their safety. I'd like to learn to worry less...

What does detachment (releasing attachments) mean to you? How do you feel about the following words: possessive, clingy, minimalist, hoarder? Do any of them resonate with you? In what way?

Example 1: I think detachment means that I should be prepared to lose people I love. Thinking about that freaks me out, even though I know it's reality even if it doesn't happen for fifty years. And, it makes me think about getting rid of junk. I think I can be clingy at times in relationships. I can also be a little bit of a hoarder...

Example 2: This is making me realize I'm probably a bit of a hoarder. I like collecting things and I have boxes and boxes of collectibles. I'm not sure why I don't sell them. I always think I'll leave them to the kids, but I don't think the kids really want them. I think detachment means I need to learn to let go of some things or be less emotionally attached. I've never been clingy in relationships though...

What types of relationships were modeled in your family? Were they out-of-balance and codependent? Or balanced and healthy?
How did they impact your views about attachment to people, things or traditions?

Example 1: I think my parents were codependent. Or, at least my mom was. She never learned to drive, and dad controlled all the money. Mom was really attached to old silverware and stuff from her parents. I think I'm really traditional like her...

Example 2: I never saw my mom in a relationship with a man. I feel like she and I have a balanced and healthy relationship. I think it's made me feel more healthy in my relationship with my husband...

What steps do you need to take to practice detachment? Detail at least five steps and prioritize them.

Remember releasing attachments allows you to love family and friends more, not less. You may want to release jealousy or control over others. You may want to let your teenagers or adult children be independent. You may want to spend meaningful time with loved ones, knowing you will not always be together.

Example 1: I really think I need to meditate on this idea of detachment. I would like to love my family more without worrying all the time. I want to clean out the garage too. I think my five steps are: 1) I need to stop calling my son to tell him to wake up for work. He is an adult. 2) I need to stop telling my daughter who she can date. She doesn't listen to me anyway...

Example 2: I really want to trust my husband to make his own decisions without second-guessing him. I want to spend more time with mom since she's getting older. I want to let my son choose his own major in school...

Imagine loving your friends and family deeply and enjoying your possessions and celebrations without being worried about losing them. Describe these experiences with all of your five senses. Now describe how you feel in your gut knowing that you are no longer worried about losing anything.

Example 1: I don't think I worry about losing things. Well, maybe just a little. I think if I had no worries at all it would be very freeing. My stomach would be more settled. My blood pressure would probably be lower. I think it looks like Christmas and smells like apple pie...

Example 2: I know I'm a big worry wort. Just thinking about not worrying makes me worry. I need to work on this. I think I would use the fancy dishes more instead of once per year. I imagine just feeling relaxed. Maybe I could pursue a hobby I like with all the time I save from worrying. I guess it would look like the beach and smell like saltwater...

Step 8: Embrace Surrender
(Lay Your Weapons Down)

"When I let go of what I am,
I become what I might be."
–Lao Tzu

We cannot realize profound joy in our lives if we demand the world gives us what we want. In the Christian faith we say, "Let go and let God." In Buddhism we embrace the wisdom of each moment. In yogic philosophy we bring our awareness to the present. I would imagine other religions and ancient teachings have similar lessons of surrender. As we practice the sweetness of letting go, we must also ask the Universe for help. We should absolutely let go, but we also need to let our intentions be known. Have you ever had a friendship or relationship with someone who thought you were a mind-reader? Perhaps they were angry and wouldn't tell you why. Don't be that person in your relationship with the world.

If the Universe doesn't know what you want, it stands to reason that neither do you. If it hasn't been articulated, more likely than not, it hasn't been defined in your own mind. As you work through this journal you will have the opportunity to identify and articulate your desires. Consider creating a vision board, starting a gratitude journal, speaking your intentions, learning to meditate, repeating affirmations, praying wisely and be ready for positive change to manifest in your life. You can achieve what you set your mind on and what you ask for. It can't be one without the other. If your dream is a secret to the Universe it cannot come to fruition.

Do the work, then relax and surrender.

Stillness practices like meditation and some forms of yoga can sometimes bring out unexpected emotions. These are typically feelings that you normally ignore rising to the surface. The benefits far outweigh the discomfort. With time, stillness and reflection can feel like a direct portal to Divine intelligence. In those moments of quiet reflection, we discover clarity and purpose.

As you grow and transform, you will elevate your environment, just like a rose planted in your window box elevates your home. I know we are all starting from different places. Just know that no matter how difficult things may be right now, what's on the other side is absolutely beautiful. Don't give up. Don't fight it. Accept it, be still, respect it, and surrender.

"When the world pushes you to your knees,
you're in the perfect position to pray."
—Rumi

What is your relationship with worry vs. faith or surrender? What do you experience most often? How do you make your desires known to the Universe?

Example 1: I think I worry more than I surrender for sure. I know I should have faith in God and I pray, but I still worry a lot...

Example 2: I have a strong faith and I don't worry much at all. I know I will be taken care of. I like to do a vision board every year to make my desires known. I also journal...

Do you believe faith and surrender are synonyms?
How would you define each?
How are they important to you?

Example 1: I think they are the same. When you have faith in God, or even in yourself, you don't worry, and you can let go. I have to work on it. I understand it intellectually, but putting it into practice in my life is different...

Example 2: I feel like for me faith is my belief in God. Surrender is more like trust. They are both important to me. But, even though I believe in God I don't always trust that things will work out...

What did you learn growing up about the idea of surrender or faith? Were there positive or negative meanings to each of those words in your family?

Example 1: Growing up, surrender really meant giving in, and that's something only weak people do. Like in sports, we were never allowed to surrender. I guess it was a negative. Faith really only had to do with Christmas time. That was when we talked about having faith...

Example 2: The church my mom went to talked a lot about faith and surrendering to Jesus, but I never liked the church. They would act like they were better than everyone and always threaten you with hell...

List five steps you will take to identify and reveal your intentions to the Universe.

Your intentions should include desires you identified in Step #4 (Love the Real You) when you created a list of things you wanted to experience before you die. It should also include talents and charitable activities you identified in Step #6 (Throw the Boomerang). Creating a vision board, starting a gratitude journal, speaking your intentions, learning to meditate, and repeating affirmations are a few ideas.

Example 1: I think I know my intentions. I want to have a happy family and work a job I really love. I want to learn to meditate, make a vision board...

Example 2: I want to go back and do more work on the other steps. I know I want to travel outside of the U.S. I think a vision board would be good, so I need to check how to make them on YouTube. I also want to make a gratitude journal...

What does a completely surrendered life look like to you? Visualize and describe what a day looks and feels like from beginning to end. Use all six senses.

Example 1: I think a completely surrendered life sounds beautiful, but also a little scary. Suppose things don't work out the way I want? I guess, that happens anyway, so it would mean when things don't work out, I don't get upset about it. Well maybe it would be relaxing afterall. Like it would look like a warm fireplace and smell like hot chocolate...

Example 2: I think being completely surrendered to the flow of life would be amazing! I would just relax and let life show me what's next instead of worrying about it. I could be calm all the time unless I was excited about something good. I think it would taste like lemonade and smell like roses...

Step 9: Wait Without Complaining
(Patience is the Truth)

"Rome wasn't built in a day."
—Proverb

It is impossible to be happy if we frequently complain. Many of us have learned that when things don't happen at our preferred pace, we should fuss about it and let the world know we disapprove. Instead of bringing desired outcomes to us, this habit creates unhappiness. Patience is accepting moments that don't feel good. These unloved moments are still the truth, whether we like them or not. I say they are the "truth" because they are happening in the moment. The experience you would prefer to have isn't actually real.

We can replace our feelings of impatience with gratitude. The fact is, we cannot see into the future and don't always know what's best for us. Delays give us a chance to prepare for whatever is coming our way. Getting too much of anything too soon is more of a curse than a gift. Without a solid foundation, dreams coming true can lead to disaster. This journal is helping you lay the groundwork, so when the time is right you are more than ready for whatever your heart desires.

When the world doesn't move at the pace you want, lean into your mindset of gratitude. Perhaps the traffic jam is keeping you safe. Maybe the long line at the grocery store is giving you a chance to listen to a podcast, catch your breath, meet someone special or notice something different. Maybe the relationship or job that you want is not right for you. You might rush into something only to later find out it was the wrong decision. There is magic in pauses. Slow down and enjoy them.

Life is full of uncertainty. It is in this place of ambiguity that we find infinite potential. Patience allows it to unfold without restriction. We learn to wait and pay attention. Our job is to open our eyes and our awareness. We can get so busy, the entire Universe is screaming to slow down, and we are too distracted to listen. We must listen before something happens to stop us in our tracks.

This doesn't mean we can never express negative feelings and vent with our close family and friends. It's normal to have frustration, and even anger, from time to time. However, it should be infrequent and for strong reasons, not a daily uncontrolled habit.

We cannot control the output in this world. We never know what the results of our efforts will be. We can only control the input. Choose to give your passion, focus and energy to the world and confidently, joyfully and patiently wait for what is to manifest.

"A setback is a setup for a comeback."
—T.D. Jakes

What is your relationship with patience vs. complaining? How do you think this relationship affects your level of happiness throughout the day?

Example 1: I think I probably complain a lot. I never thought about it before. When things get screwed up and I feel helpless, I complain to anyone who will listen. It's not really a happy feeling at all...

Example 2: I think I'm pretty patient, but I worry I don't speak my mind and I let people take advantage of me. Maybe I need to work more on my self-love...

What does patience mean to you?
How do you feel when you're around people who are impatient or complaining?

Example 1: Honestly, I find it scary when I'm around impatient people. My dad was always an aggressive driver. He would curse and honk and it was terrible to be around him...

Example 2: I think everyone I know complains all the time so it's pretty normal to me. It's almost fun, but at the same time, my friends aren't really doing anything with their lives...

When you were growing up, did your parents or guardians complain? Were they patient? How did this impact you?

Example 1: My mother used to complain from sun up to sun down. Nothing ever worked out for her. I think I got the same habit from her. When things don't work out I always blame someone else...

Example 2: I was raised by my aunt and she was always really patient with me. I think because she knew what I went through with my mom. Her patience made me feel really loved...

What steps will you take to become more patient? What mental habits can you create to replace moments of impatience? How will you incorporate gratitude?

Example 1: I think if I count backwards from five when I'm annoyed, I can be more patient. Also, when I'm waiting, I can just look at my cell phone and catch up on the news and stuff...

Example 2: I think learning to meditate regularly will help me to be more patient. When I'm in traffic I will be grateful that I'm not the reason for the traffic...

Take a moment and imagine a month in your life where you don't complain or expect things to be different. You are grateful for things as they are. Now use all your senses. What do you see, hear, feel, think, smell, taste? How's your gut?

Example 1: Hmmm. A whole month without complaining sounds interesting. I can't even imagine just accepting it when things don't go right. Well, I think it would be pretty peaceful. I would feel grateful, and that would make me feel happier. I think it smells like beer and tacos because I'd just be going with the flow...

Example 2: I hardly complain as it is. If I really focused on being patient I think I'd have a really relaxing month. It would smell like the spa, like lavender. I think it would sound like string instruments. My gut would feel really relaxed...

Step 10: Elevate Your Compassion
(Don't Eat the Dead)

"The living shouldn't eat the dead."
–Unknown

Your level of happiness will skyrocket when you stop harming others, directly or indirectly. This is part of Universal law and justice. Just as in the laws created by people, gross negligence is a crime, and ignorance is not a defense. When we don't respect all sentient beings and the living environment around us, we create unanticipated problems. Whether they are infectious diseases like COVID-19 or E. coli, lifestyle diseases like diabetes or heart disease, the global climate crisis, homelessness or crime, every action creates a reaction. We cannot harm others, intentionally or innocently, and walk away unscathed.

Most of us think we don't harm others often. Here are a few areas where we may inadvertently hurt others: teasing or shaming, yelling or bullying, watching pornography, meat and dairy consumption, use of animal products like wool or leather, and use of products tested on abused and tormented animals.

Martin Luther King Jr. famously said, "Injustice anywhere is a threat to justice everywhere." If we didn't think it was okay to torture and abuse animals, we wouldn't graduate to doing the same to people.

Imagine the opposite of a society built on violence and inhumanity. Imagine a world where every soul was self-actualized, every animal had a right to live, and all men and women were equal regardless of race, class, background, sexual orientation or identity. The only way to create this type of world is to change ourselves.

The physical health benefits of a whole food, plant-based vegan lifestyle are widely documented. The emotional and spiritual benefits are beyond words. Just because we have the power to control, oppress and harm other people or animals doesn't mean we should. The Garden of Eden, God's paradise for people, was vegan.

The more you move away from violence and reclaim compassion, the happier you will become.

"I've learned that people will forget what you said, people will forget what you did, but people will never forget how you made them feel."
—Maya Angelou

How do you feel about your current level of compassion? Are you able to empathize with the situations and emotions of people of different races, nationalities, socioeconomic backgrounds and sexual orientation or identity? Do you have compassion for animals that are not pets, like cows, pigs, chickens, fish or bees? What areas need more work?

Example 1: I think I have a lot of compassion for my family and friends but not as much for other people. I don't know much about other types of people. I grew up on a farm and I know I have compassion for farm animals, but I still eat them. I guess I can work on learning about other cultures and maybe eat less meat...

Example 2: I have a lot of compassion for poor and disadvantaged children, but not adults. I think I need to work on that. I don't eat any animals, but I could probably work on not killing so many insects for no reason, like when they're just outside...

What does a compassionate life mean for you? Describe a time when you felt deep empathy or mercy. Think back to your childhood if necessary.

Example 1: I remember when I was a little kid I used to pick up the worms that fell from trees after the rain. I don't do that anymore, but it was so cute that I actually cared about the little worms...

Example 2: I think a compassionate life would mean I spent more time thinking about how the things I do impact people, or impact the whole county. I remember when I was little I always worried about the old lady who's husband died. I used to help her carry her groceries. Helping her made me feel good...

Did you ever hear the word "compassion" when you were growing up? How did your family or community show empathy to people who were different from them? In what ways did they show compassion to animals? How did these experiences impact you?

Example 1: My dad was always saving animals when I was a kid. I remember he brought home a three-legged dog one day, and a sick bird another time. At church, we always took a collection for refugees. I don't remember the word compassion though...

Example 2: Growing up we never thought too much about other people. My parents were really focused on the family and nobody thought about animals at all...

What steps are you willing to take to lead a more compassionate life?
Give at least five examples and be specific.

Example 1: I think I can be kinder. I can give a little money when I see someone needs help. I can donate a little more to charity. I can give better gifts to the teachers at school or help out more...

Example 2: I really think I want to try becoming a vegetarian. That should count as five! Lol! I'll be giving up pork, beef, chicken and fish. But seriously, I think I can also start tithing at church...

Close your eyes for a few moments and imagine a world where everyone is treated with dignity, respect and compassion, even small animals. Experience this world through all of your senses. Now, open your eyes and record what you experienced. What did you see, smell, feel, taste and hear? Did your body tense up or relax when you visualized a compassionate world?

Example 1: It's really nice to imagine a compassionate world. My body got really relaxed. I imagine it smells like cut grass and fresh flowers. I saw children playing and heard an ice-cream truck...

Example 2: I imagined neighbors looking out for each other and needing less guns. I imagined people eating more fruits and vegetables and being healthier. My body felt calm. It's smelled like watermelon and looked like a sun shower...

Step 11: Work with Passion
(Work Equals Play)

"I would rather die of passion than of boredom."
–Vincent Van Gogh

When you engage in enjoyable, challenging work on a consistent basis, you will grow in happiness. Even if you are working full-time or are busy raising children, finding a few hours a week to focus on your passions is critical. As we build on this idea, your work in Steps #4 and #6 (Love the Real You and Throw the Boomerang) will once again come into play. Identifying your passions and releasing them into the world are crucial for assembling a life where you can work with passion and purpose.

The late poet, Mary Oliver asked, "Are you breathing just a little and calling it a life?" Are you doing your best work or just playing it safe? Work equaling play doesn't mean you can't be a waiter or a street-sweeper. You can do any honest work that pays the bills and supports your home. However, you must engage in work you genuinely enjoy that challenges you on a consistent basis, even if it's not your paying job.

Martin Luther King Jr. said, "If a man is called to be a street sweeper...he should sweep the streets so well that all the hosts of heaven and earth will pause to say, 'here lived a great street sweeper who did his job well.'" If you think sweeping streets isn't challenging, try it. It is as important as any job.

Even simple and seemingly mundane work can be performed with love and passion. I realize not everyone is able to quit their job and become an actor, a singer or a comedian. Or can they? We cling to a perception of safety that isn't real. We think if we have the house, the car, the spouse or the stuff we will be protected from pain, when, in reality, the pain will greet us regardless of the lavish gates we build to avoid it. In the meantime, how should we live our lives? Should we hoard our fear along with our sweaters, old shoes and paperback books? Now don't go running to work in the morning to quit your job. However, as you release attachments through your work in Step #7 (Learn to Detach) you may find your life becomes more spacious and flexible, and then, who knows what shifts may come your way.

Reinventing your existing job, changing employers or careers, pursuing self-employment, taking on new hobbies and volunteering are a few ways to make work equal play in your life. Being in the zone or "flow" is a blissful state of immersion and heightened focus. It's how you feel when you are so engrossed in an enjoyable project, you lose track of time. It's an excellent indicator of working with passion. The more time you spend in the zone, the happier you will be.

"Work is love made visible."
—Kahlil Gibran

Where are you on your journey towards identifying and following your life's purpose? What do you care about most in this world (not including family and friends)? What would be your dream job if you didn't have to make a living. *Don't be cautious, really dream!*

Example 1: I'm still trying to figure out my purpose, but I think I'm getting closer. I realize exercise is really important to me. I really care about kids with autism because of my two daughters. Maybe my dream job would be working as an exercise instructor for kids with autism...

Example 2: I'm sure my purpose has something to do with traveling. I've always loved seeing the world. I really love working as a nurse, though. Maybe my dream job would be working as a nurse in another country...

What does passion mean to you as it relates to either paid or volunteer work? Name at least five activities that you enjoy and get so wrapped up in you lose track of time. Consider the activities you identified in Step #4 (Love the Real You) that you haven't done yet.

Example 1: I'm really passionate about the work I do with my local food bank. I think everyone should have food to eat, especially kids. I lose track of time when I'm watching TV, singing and cooking. One of my bucket list activities is to take a cooking class. I wonder if I could do a cooking class for kids who are hungry...

Example 2: I really enjoy riding my bike, dancing, swimming, doing crochet and throwing parties for my friends. I feel like I'm passionate about all of that. My bucket list has a wedding in Spain, maybe I should turn that into a party for my friends. We could bike the countryside...

Who do you know in your family or community who clearly loves their employment or their volunteer work? How do you feel when you're around them? How have they impacted you?

Example 1: My son's teacher is always really excited about her class. Her enthusiasm really makes her a great teacher. The kids and the parents can feel it. I think it makes everyone work harder and feel proud about the school...

Example 2: The owner of my hair salon is always so excited about doing hair. It just blows me away. It seems like really hard work to me, but she always seems so happy it's contagious. It makes me want to be around her...

What steps can you take to work in areas that you care the most about? Think about trauma or difficulty from Step #1 that you can use for something positive. Who are you uniquely qualified to help? Do you need more education, insight, skills, practice or connections? How can you obtain any missing pieces? What's your timeframe?

Example 1: I grew up with alcoholic parents, so I think I really understand what it feels like to be neglected as a kid. I'd really like to help teenagers learn to believe in themselves. I think the first thing to do is reach out to some local high schools and see if I can volunteer. I can do that this month. By the end of six months, I think I'll know if this is the right path for me...

Example 2: I still need to work on some of the trauma I've experienced in my life. I don't think I'm ready to work in that area. I really enjoy volunteering as an adult literacy tutor at the library. Everyone should be able to read and understand ideas. I'm going to look at ways to do more work with literacy. I'll call the library director tomorrow and see what she thinks...

Close your eyes. Imagine consistently doing work that is deeply fulfilling and in service to others. Experience all of your senses, including your gut. How do you feel? What do you see, hear, taste and smell?

Example 1: When I closed my eyes, I imagined teaching dance in low-income communities. It felt really relaxing to go back to a community I can relate to and bring something to give hope. I saw little kids smiling and heard laughter. My stomach was a little tight going back to the old neighborhood. It smelled like iced tea and sweat...

Example 2: I imagined creating a curriculum to teach high school girls to love themselves and going all around my state to implement it. I felt so relaxed. I think I smiled the whole time my eyes were closed. It smelled like hairspray and rainwater. I felt really warm. I heard the girls laughing at my jokes...

Step 12: Fly Free!
(Float Like a Butterfly)

"I am the greatest. I said that even before I knew I was."
–Muhammad Ali

We cannot experience mind-blowing happiness if we do not feel free. Long before affirmations became part of the language of popular self-help culture, Muhammad Ali had the foresight to tell the world he was the greatest of all time. That takes courage. I'm sure he had moments of doubt, we all do, but he did the work, stuck to his story and watched it manifest. No matter what you think of boxing, he was a man with an undeniable sense of freedom.

The floating butterfly seems to move effortlessly because it's going with the flow of the air and its own unique abilities. In other words, it's flowing with life. It's in the zone. When you look closely, you may notice the butterfly doesn't flap its wings. Rather, it contracts its body and makes a figure eight with them as if it's dancing. We can dance too. Dancing while we heal and work. Dancing in community, generosity, compassion and spirit. Dancing in authenticity and self-love. Dancing while letting go and while waiting. Dancing while we create our vision.

The decision to be joyful is exactly that, a decision. I know if you don't have food, shelter or safety, dancing won't be your first priority. I know when you have lost a loved one, especially through violence, the trauma is deep, and the scars linger. I pray that you find healing not only in my words, but in the tools that I've shared with you. I hope you can see some light at the end of the long tunnel.

It's easier to dance when you have hope. When you have a roadmap. When you know what your passions are. When you've identified the things that make you happy. I hope you've found some, if not all of that here. When the sparks come together and connect, Bam!— Mind blown! Maybe you've felt the explosion, maybe not. It's huge and it takes time. It may happen as one big blast or many small ones. Either way, you'll know it when you feel it.

From the day we are born, society tells us whether we should be dressed in pink or blue, if we should drink our mother's milk or a concoction from someone else's mother, what and whose body we should eat, what we need to know, what we should believe, where we can live, who we can love, and on and on. Our society tells us who we are and who it thinks we should be.

When we learn to follow our own innate set of skills, talents and passions, we learn to float. Life gets easier. Goals become attainable. As we've learned in the Steps, there are things we need to release to be happy. We must heal from our past, stop harming ourselves and others, and let go of anger, attachment and greed. In this releasing we discover that we feel good. We reach toward the things that will raise our consciousness and make us feel even better: recognizing our own unique spirit, creating community, learning to love our authentic self, expanding our generosity, asking for help, developing patience and working with joy and enthusiasm.

Now's the time to pull everything together into a sustainable self-love and self-care practice that you can enjoy for many years. Incorporate regular exercise and time for stillness and reflection. Take care of your body. We can't attain mind-blowing happiness if we're damaging ourselves with alcohol, tobacco, drugs, poor nutrition or lack of rest. Now it's time to enjoy the sweetness of life. Improving every day and forgiving ourselves when we stumble. Speaking kindly to ourselves even if we're the only person to do so. Taking baths. Taking naps. Anointing ourselves with fragrant oils. Knowing we are good and worthy. Living without guilt or regrets. Feeling the warmth of a loving heart each morning when we rise. This is mind-blowing happiness.

*"Freeing yourself was one thing; claiming ownership
of that freed self was another."*
—*Toni Morrison*

How free do you feel in your day-to-day life?
If life were a path to full expression of self,
where would you be on your journey?

Example 1: I really don't feel free at all. I have work and family obligations all the time. I guess I'm at the beginning of my journey to freedom. I love my family but I need to set better boundaries. As for work, I need to start thinking about other career paths...

Example 2: I feel pretty free in my life. I love the work that I do, but I think I can do some weekend activities to really identify my passions. I think I know what I like, but I'll know better when I actually do it. Like, I know I like running, but I don't know if I like it enough to do it all the time...

Is freedom important to you? Why?
Name at least five activities that make you feel free.
How do you reconcile freedom with choice and
responsibility? Can they all coexist?

Example 1: Even though I feel trapped a lot of the time, I think freedom is important to me. I think it's what everyone wants. I feel free when I can take a nap without anyone bothering me. I feel free when I can go shopping by myself with my own money. I feel free when I can have a girl's night out with my friends. I can have moments of freedom while still being responsible for my kids and my husband...

Example 2: I really want to run away from my life. I don't think I was ready to start a family so young, and being a single parent is exhausting. I don't think I can be free until the little one is at least twelve or so. I feel a little free when everyone's at school and I'm at work, but then it's still work so... I made my choices...

In what ways was the idea of freedom discussed in your family? Who do you know either personally or through media/celebrity that seem to be free in a way that appeals to you?

Example 1: My family never talked about freedom. We were told to get a job with benefits so we could survive. Oprah always seems really free to me. She never had children or got married. I'm not sure if I ever want kids, so I guess that appeals to me...

Example 2: Growing up, my mom always said I could do anything I set my mind to, so that felt really freeing for me. I've always wanted to be taken care of, so when I see some of the reality show housewives or celebrity wives, it looks freeing to me. They don't have to worry about money...

Name at least five steps you can take to achieve freedom in your own life without shirking your responsibilities.

Example 1: I think getting the kids on a schedule is one way to get more freedom. And, I want to go back to school so I can get a better paying job. Learning to say "no" more often would help. I think if I got up earlier, I'd have more quiet time for me...

Example 2: I really want to get a job where I don't have to go into an office, so I want to look for remote work. I'm going to start this weekend. That would give me a lot more freedom. I also want to talk to my neighbors about carpooling the kids to school...

Take a few moments to imagine a life where you really feel the freedom of the *12 Steps to Mind-Blowing Happiness*. Incorporate all your senses.

Example 1: Wow. That's a lot. I'd be feeling whole and healed, have a great community and spiritual life, I wouldn't be angry or frustrated, I would really love my authentic self. I'd know what my talents are and I'd share them freely. I wouldn't be so attached to everything. I'd be patient and I wouldn't worry. I'd have faith and more compassion. I'd be engaged in my passion and I'd feel free! Taking a few moments to imagine a life like that puts such a smile on my face. I can feel the warm sun on my cheeks. I smell honeysuckle. I hear reggae music. It's pure joy...

Example 2: It's hard for me to imagine everything falling into place. I'm sure it would take years. I was able to imagine having a good job in an office that I like that pays my bills and repairing my relationship with my mom. Those two things alone brought tears to my eyes. My stomach felt so soft. All my muscles relaxed. I could hear birds singing...

Organic Synergy
(Bringing it Together)

"If you look at the people in your circle and don't get inspired,
then you don't have a circle. You have a cage."
–Nipsey Hussle

Synergy is defined as when the whole is greater than the sum of its parts. Organic Synergy is when the magic of synergy happens naturally and joyfully, like a sunrise or a flower growing. There is incredible power, but there is no fight. The *12 Steps to Mind-Blowing Happiness* work in synergy, creating a result that is far more than the individual components. As you incorporate the Steps into your life on a consistent basis, you will exponentially increase your level of joy and fulfillment. Things you hadn't even thought about will begin to fall into place. Learning and using the Steps will create positive change in your life in more ways than you can count or name. Use the tools in this section to help bring the pieces together. Enjoy your journey with the Steps, and revisit them often as they work together to bring mind-blowing happiness into your life!

Describe how you expect this concept of Organic Synergy to work in your life. What are your most powerful takeaways from the *12 Steps to Mind-Blowing Happiness?*

Example 1: I can see where the Steps overlap. Like getting rid of anger also helps me to be more patient. And, being more authentic makes it easier for me to join groups. My biggest takeaway is I really need to work on myself if I want my life to get better...

Example 2: I think Organic Synergy makes sense because things start to work together. Like if you stop eating meat, you probably get healthier. And, if you spend more time doing work you enjoy, you become kinder and more patient. My biggest takeaway is the part about anger. I always thought anger was necessary, but now I see I can work to get rid of it, because I have never made a good decision while I was angry...

Mind-Blowing Happiness Assessment Quiz

Try this quiz on yourself, on friends and on family members. After taking an initial assessment, focus on the action steps you created in your journaling exercises, then try the quiz again. Over time, you will see your rating improve. Rate each Step on a scale from 1-10, 10 being *mind-blowing mastery*, and 1 being *needs a lot of work*. Use a separate sheet to take the quiz for different people.

Step	Scale
Healing	1 – 2 – 3 – 4 – 5 – 6 – 7 – 8 – 9 – 10
Spirituality	1 – 2 – 3 – 4 – 5 – 6 – 7 – 8 – 9 – 10
Connection & Community	1 – 2 – 3 – 4 – 5 – 6 – 7 – 8 – 9 – 10
Authenticity & Self-Love	1 – 2 – 3 – 4 – 5 – 6 – 7 – 8 – 9 – 10
Releasing Anger/Peacefulness	1 – 2 – 3 – 4 – 5 – 6 – 7 – 8 – 9 – 10
Generosity	1 – 2 – 3 – 4 – 5 – 6 – 7 – 8 – 9 – 10
Detachment	1 – 2 – 3 – 4 – 5 – 6 – 7 – 8 – 9 – 10
Surrender	1 – 2 – 3 – 4 – 5 – 6 – 7 – 8 – 9 – 10
Patience	1 – 2 – 3 – 4 – 5 – 6 – 7 – 8 – 9 – 10
Compassion	1 – 2 – 3 – 4 – 5 – 6 – 7 – 8 – 9 – 10
Working with Passion	1 – 2 – 3 – 4 – 5 – 6 – 7 – 8 – 9 – 10
Freedom	1 – 2 – 3 – 4 – 5 – 6 – 7 – 8 – 9 – 10

Total your numbers for a final score. _____

Assessing Your Happiness Scores

12-59: Your happiness quotient needs some work. You are not alone. The good news is you have this journal. If you don't already have *Thinking Outside the Chrysalis: A Black Woman's Guide to Spreading Her Wings*, purchase a copy for additional support. If you find yourself feeling depressed or overwhelmed, get counseling from a certified mental health professional. Feelings cannot destroy you. You can become happier. Stay the course.

60-84: You're in the middle of the pack, not quite loving life, but keeping the pieces together. You've got lots of company. Keep doing the work, and you will see progress. Life is about to get a lot better. Don't give up!

85-107: Look at you, smiling like you've got a secret! You are well on your way to happiness of the mind-blowing variety. Work your magic. Use all the tools. Keep up the great work! Your journey is getting super-juicy!

108-120: Congratulations! If you are in this range, you have obtained mind-blowing happiness! Continue to pay attention to the Steps to maintain this beautiful achievement and stay in "the zone." You will find people are drawn to you. Make sure to generously share what you've learned!

Relationship Assessment Quiz

Your relationships with family and friends have a huge impact on your happiness. A useful way to assess relationships in your life is to use the Eight Main Life Areas. Identify a person in your life, perhaps a spouse or life partner, love interest, friend or family member. Being on "the same level" means you take a similar approach or have a compatible background in that area. Don't overthink your answers. Use a separate sheet to take the quiz for different people.

Life Area	On the same level?
1. Mental health/personal development	Rarely/Sometimes/Often
2. Relationships	Rarely/Sometimes/Often
3. Physical health	Rarely/Sometimes/Often
4. Spiritual life	Rarely/Sometimes/Often
5. Occupation	Rarely/Sometimes/Often
6. Fun and recreation	Rarely/Sometimes/Often
7. Money	Rarely/Sometimes/Often
8. Physical environment (home/work)	Rarely/Sometimes/Often

Score: 1 for Rarely – 3 for Sometimes – 5 for Often

Tally up your scores. _____

Assessing Your Relationship Scores

8-20: Scores in this range show a low level of compatibility in lifestyle and world view and may cause contention and discord. Relationships in this score range often need help, or they may devolve into silence, misunderstanding and disconnect. If this is a relationship you want to maintain you may want to consider additional support from a qualified therapist or counselor.

21-30: Scores in this range show a healthy level of compatibility with plenty of room for growth. Continue to stay connected and share interests and time. Discuss ideas. Communicate feelings. You may want to share some of the *12 Steps to Mind-Blowing Happiness* as a place to grow from.

31-40: Scores in this range show a deep level of compatibility. These scores usually appear in long, deep relationships, close family ties, or relationships that are naturally aligned. Enjoy and treasure these strong connections.

Important Note:

The assessment quiz is for information only and is not a replacement for a consultation with a qualified counselor. Please be aware that it is possible for a dysfunctional relationship to score well. The quiz does not test for things like emotional or physical abuse. It simply tests for alignment across the Eight Main Life Areas. It provides a window of understanding into the way you relate with other people in your life.

Also by

Trish Ahjel Roberts

Thinking Outside the Chrysalis:
A Black Woman's Guide to Spreading Her Wings
(a self-help memoir)

Chocolate Soufflé
(a novel)

Mind-Blowing Happiness™ Guide to Self-Care
(e-book)

HOW DID
12 STEPS TO MIND-BLOWING HAPPINESS
CHANGE YOUR LIFE?

Share your story for the chance to win
a FREE gift!

Email: hello@trishahjelroberts.com

Winners drawn monthly.

_____

_____

_____

Subscribe to

The Mind-Blowing Happiness™ Podcast

For weekly topics, tips and inspiration
to juice up your life's journey!

BRING
THE POWER OF TRANSFORMATION
TO YOUR ORGANIZATION

Invite Trish Ahjel Roberts
to speak at your event!

Visit TrishAhjelRoberts.com/speaking.

_____

_____

_____

Follow Trish Ahjel Roberts on social media!

IG: @trishahjelroberts
FB: @trishahjelroberts
Twitter: @trishahjel
YouTube: Trish Ahjel Roberts

About the Author

Trish Ahjel Roberts has made it her mission to inspire and empower you to live with passion and purpose to reach your fullest potential. She is a self-actualization coach, yoga and meditation instructor, reiki practitioner, plant-based retreat organizer and founder of Mind-Blowing Happiness LLC and Black Vegan Life™. She was born and raised in Brooklyn, NY and attended Stuyvesant High School in Manhattan. She holds a bachelor's degree from the Metropolitan College of New York and an MBA from Long Island University. After years of working as a financial advisor with many unhappy, but wealthy, clients, she quit her corporate job to share her 12-step approach to a self-actualized life. She is the author of three self-help books: the e-book, *Mind-Blowing Happiness™ Guide to Self-Care;* the self-help memoir, *Thinking Outside the Chrysalis: A Black Woman's Guide to Spreading Her Wings;* and the inspirational journal, *12 Steps to Mind-Blowing Happiness: A Journal of Insights, Quotes & Questions to Juice Up Your Journey.* She is also the author of the #sexyfunnysmart romantic drama, *Chocolate Soufflé.* She has more than a decade of Buddhist study at Kadampa Meditation Center in Atlanta, GA and has practiced yoga for more than twenty years. She lives with her daughter and their dog, @vegan_cavachon, in Atlanta and travels the world helping people amplify their voice, open their heart and step into their power. She believes movement and nature are therapy and loves hiking, running, hot yoga and anything on the beach.

Resources

Eight Main Life Areas

⁕ *Mental health and personal development*
Self-awareness and mental wellness, as well as the level of interest in improving ourselves

⁕ *Relationships*
Partners and love interests, family, friends, co-workers and acquaintances

⁕ *Physical health*
Health of the physical body and activities related to maintain wellness like exercise or visiting a doctor regularly

⁕ *Spiritual life*
Any religious affiliations and activities like attending a church, mosque or temple. It also includes activities to explore your Divine consciousness like yoga and meditation.

⁕ *Occupation*
Usually paid employment, but also unpaid work like maintaining a household or significant volunteer work

⁕ *Fun and recreation*
Enjoyable hobbies and activities

⁕ *Money*
Financial circumstances and perspective

⁕ *Physical environment (home/work)*
Work space (office, warehouse, outdoors, neighborhood etc.) and home space (house, apartment, neighborhood, etc.)

Deepening Self-Love—Meet the Love MOB

Without question, love is your birthright—it is the purest and most beneficial of emotions. Your early experiences with love, what I like to call your Love MOB, establish the foundation for self-love. The MOB consists of Mothers, Others and Brothers:

* Your biological Mother and other mother figures offer your initiation into the nurturing sweetness of love.
* Others refers to your other-worldly experiences of a loving God or organized Universe that provides a sense of structural safety in the world.
* Brothers are your extended family and community that expands your network of love and support far and wide.

This powerful foundation helps you develop the Pillars of Self-Love:

* Self-Awareness
* Authenticity
* Confidence
* Healthy Boundaries

If you grew up in a generation where children were "seen and not heard," being self-aware takes some practice. Self-awareness arises when we are encouraged to be reflective. You might be asked, "How do you feel?" or "What do you think about that?" Authenticity stems from both self-knowledge and acceptance. From this safe footing, you can be honest with others and yourself. Confidence builds upon that, enabling you to speak your mind knowing you can learn and make corrections as needed. With these structures in place, healthy boundaries become natural, allowing you to protect your mind, body and spirit from those who might do you harm.

What was your childhood experience like with the Love MOB? How strong are your pillars of self-love (Self-awareness, Authenticity, Confidence and Healthy Boundaries)? Where do you need work? What can you do to strengthen your sense of self-love?

Characters in The Rib King

1914 — Mr. Sitwell — groundskeeper
The Barclays — foster parents (Herbert)
Ms. Mamie — the cook
14/15 year old orphans — Jennie, Mabel
Frederick — three wells on left cheek
Mack — lose part of right ear
Bart — potbell.
Mr. Boudreau — Mamie's predecessor
people Jennie, Jean, handyman (smiled a lot)
Petunia, Jennie's predecessor
Mrs. Lawson — parlor maid
Wash Talbot — Florida
(Gary nephew)
Cherokee Red
Billy — nephew, boarding house
owner

pneumonia

Dr. Corbet NIH — Covid Vaccine
team

Stanford Center on Longevity
Emma Thompson & her motto in the mouse

Step #1 –Healing

- TrishAhjelRoberts.com/resources for music, meditations and affirmations for healing
- *Thinking Outside the Chrysalis: A Black Woman's Guide to Spreading Her Wings* by Trish Ahjel Roberts
- *My Grandmother's Hands: Racialized Trauma and the Pathway to Mending Our Hearts and Bodies* by Resmaa Menakem
- *The Courage to Heal* by Ellen Bass and Laura Davis
- *The Body Keeps the Score* by Bessel Van Der Kolk, MD
- *Healing the Fragmented Selves of Trauma Survivors* by Janina Fisher
- *Get Over It!: Thought Therapy for Healing the Hard Stuff* by Iyanla Vanzant
- TherapyforBlackgirls.com
- Psychologytoday.com
- Betterhelp.com
- Zocdoc.com

Step #2 –Spirituality

- TrishAhjelRoberts.com/resources for music, meditations and affirmations for spirit
- *Thinking Outside the Chrysalis: A Black Woman's Guide to Spreading Her Wings* by Trish Ahjel Roberts
- *How to Solve Our Human Problems* by Geshe Kelsang Gyatso
- *The Wisdom of Sundays: Life-Changing Insights from Super Soul Conversations* by Oprah Winfrey
- *The Yamas and Niyamas* by Deborah Adele
- *Bhagavad Gita: A New Translation* by Stephen Mitchell
- *Seven Laws of Spiritual Success* by Deepak Choprah
- *Introduction to Buddhism* by Geshe Kelsang Gyatso
- *Being Supernatural* by Dr. Joe Dispenza
- *The Road Less Traveled* by M. Scott Peck, M.D.
- *Teachings of the Master: The Collected Sayings of Jesus Christ,* compiled by Philip Law
- The New Living Translation Bible
- Kadampa.org
- UCC.org
- howtoTYL.com/us
- modernbuddhism.com

Step #3 —Connection

- TrishAhjelRoberts.com/resources for music, meditations and affirmations for connection
- Meetup.com is my favorite resource for finding groups of like-minded folks who want to meet in person.
- Facebook groups and events are also very good for online interactions as well as in-person.
- Eventbrite is also a good place to search for local events.
- Charitable organizations (local and national non-profits, social justice organizations, food banks, etc.) Helping others is empowering and makes you a better and happier person.
- Physical (fitness center, YMCA, yoga studio, etc.)
- Spiritual (church, temple, meditation center, mosque, ashram, etc.)
- Affinity (LGBTQ, vegan, Caribbean, girls' night out, Black moms, etc.)
- Hobby (walking, knitting, dancing, card games, etc.)
- Intellectual (discussion groups, book clubs, career or personal development, leadership, political, etc.)

Step #4 —Authenticity & Self-Love

- TrishAhjelRoberts.com/resources for music, meditations and affirmations for self-love
- *Thinking Outside the Chrysalis: A Black Woman's Guide to Spreading Her Wings* by Trish Ahjel Roberts
- *I Know Why the Caged Bird Sings* by Maya Angelou
- *We're Going to Need More Wine* by Gabrielle Union
- *Becoming* by Michelle Obama
- *Born a Crime* by Trevor Noah
- *And Still I Rise: A Book of Poems* by Maya Angelou

Step #5 —Peace

- TrishAhjelRoberts.com/resources for music, meditations and affirmations for peace
- *Thinking Outside the Chrysalis: A Black Woman's Guide to Spreading Her Wings* by Trish Ahjel Roberts

- *My Grandmother's Hands: Racialized Trauma and the Pathway to Mending Our Hearts and Bodies* by Resmaa Menakem
- *Universal Compassion* by Geshe Kelsang Gyatso
- Kadampa.org

Step #6 –Generosity

- TrishAhjelRoberts.com/resources for music, meditations and affirmations for generosity
- *Thinking Outside the Chrysalis: A Black Woman's Guide to Spreading Her Wings* by Trish Ahjel Roberts
- Charity begins at home. Reach out to friends and neighbors who might need help, perhaps a single mom or senior citizen. A small gift or card can mean a lot to someone who's having a difficult time. If you are able, add money or a gift card inside of a note. If the receiver indicates they don't need money, encourage them to "pay it forward" and donate to another person or cause.
- Consider putting together care bundles for homeless people with snacks, drinks, toiletries, socks or cash.
- Consider putting a few dollars in a card for essential workers.
- Tip restaurant servers and delivery people generously.
- Consider buying something for the person behind you in line at the drive-through or in line at the grocery store.
- If someone asks for your help, do your best to find a way to say "yes." Don't put yourself in an unsafe position, but do what you can when you are able.
- *Super Rich* by Russell Simmons
- Support national and local charities with donations or by volunteering. Some of my favorites are local food pantries, local domestic violence or homeless shelters, animal rights organizations (The Humane League, Mercy for Animals, PETA), animal sanctuaries, social justice organizations (Untilfreedom.com, Grassrootslaw.com, Blacklivesmatter.com), progressive political organizations (Cobb County Progressives, Democratic Party), women and children's charities (Dress for Success, St. Jude's Hospital, The Junior League), Habitat for Humanity, and finally give away some stuff (Goodwill, Salvation Army)

Step #7 –Detachment

- TrishAhjelRoberts.com/resources for music, meditations and affirmations for detachment
- *Thinking Outside the Chrysalis: A Black Woman's Guide to Spreading Her Wings* by Trish Ahjel Roberts
- *Introduction to Buddhism* by Geshe Kelsang Gyatso
- *Transform Your Life* by Geshe Kelsang Gyatso
- *How to Solve Our Human Problems* by Geshe Kelsang Gyatso
- *Happy.* Directed by Roko Belic. Wadi Rum Productions, 2011.
- *Minimalism: A Documentary About the Important Things.* Directed by Matt D'Avelia. Catalyst Films, 2016.
- *The True Cost.* Directed by Andrew Morgan. Untold Creative, 2015.
- *Tidying Up* by Marie Kondo

Step #8 –Surrender

- TrishAhjelRoberts.com/resources for music, meditations and affirmations for surrender
- *Thinking Outside the Chrysalis: A Black Woman's Guide to Spreading Her Wings* by Trish Ahjel Roberts
- *How to Solve Our Human Problems* by Geshe Kelsang Gyatso
- Choprameditation.com
- Dr. Joe Dispenza. Tuning in to New Potentials, 2014 (meditation album)
- *Becoming Supernatural: How Common People are Doing the Uncommon* by Dr. Joe Dispenza
- *Beyond the Secret: The Awakening. Directed* by Melinda Boyer. The Hollywood Effect, 2020.
- *Eat, Pray, Love.* Directed by Ryan Murphy. Starring Julia Roberts. Columbia Pictures, 2010.
- *The Secret.* Directed by Drew Heriot. Documentary. Prime Time Productions, 2006.
- Chitrasukhu.com
- Traceeyoga.com
- Recommended Apps: Oprah & Deepak 21-Day Meditation Experience, Louise Hay Affirmations, Calm, Insight Timer

Step #9 –Patience

- TrishAhjelRoberts.com/resources for music, meditations and affirmations for patience
- *Thinking Outside the Chrysalis: A Black Woman's Guide to Spreading Her Wings* by Trish Ahjel Roberts
- *How to Solve Our Human Problems* by Geshe Kelsang Gyatso
- Dr. Joe Dispenza. *Tuning in to New Potentials,* 2014 (meditation album)
- *Becoming Supernatural: How Common People are Doing the Uncommon* by Dr. Joe Dispenza
- *The Pursuit of Happyness.* Directed by Gabriele Muccino. Starring Will Smith and Jaden Smith. Columbia Pictures, 2006.
- Kadampa.org
- Choprameditation.com
- Recommended Apps: Oprah & Deepak 21-Day Meditation Experience, Louise Hay Affirmations, Calm, Insight Timer

Step #10 –Compassion

- TrishAhjelRoberts.com/resources for music, meditations and affirmations for compassion
- *Thinking Outside the Chrysalis: A Black Woman's Guide to Spreading Her Wings* by Trish Ahjel Roberts
- *The Game Changers.* Directed by Louie Psihoyos. Starring James Wilks. Game Changers Film, 2019.
- *Vegucated.* Directed by Marisa Miller Wolfson. Starring Tesla Lobo. Get Vegucated, 2011.
- *My Grandmother's Hands: Racialized Trauma and the Pathway to Mending Our Hearts and Bodies* by Resmaa Menakem
- *Universal Compassion* by Gelse Kelsang Gyatso
- *Sistah Vegan.* Edited by A. Breeze Harper
- *By Any Greens Necessary* by Tracye Lynn McQuirter
- *Skinny Bitch* by Rory Freedman
- *Addict Nation: An Intervention for America* by Jane Velez-Mitchell
- *We Are One.* Directed by Kevin Mukherji. Featuring Forest Whitaker. Carlos Sanz Production, 2017.

- *The Post-Traumatic Slave Diet.* Featuring Dr. Milton Mills. Karen Boone Production, 2016.
- *Cowspiracy: The Sustainability Secret.* Directed by Kip Anderson. Starring Kip Anderson. Appian Way, 2016.
- *Lovelace.* Directed by Rob Epstein. Starring Amanda Seyfried. Nu Image, 2013.
- *Earthlings.* Directed by Shaun Monson. Narrated by Joaquin Phoenix. Nation Earth, 2005.
- *Let Plants Nourish You* by D. Natasha "Chef Beee" Brewley
- *Veganize and Heal Your Life* by Neeta Sanders
- *The Prevent and Reverse Heart Disease Cookbook* by Ann Crile Esselstyn and Jane Esselstyn
- *The Greenprint: Plant-Based Diet, Best Body, Better World* by Marco Borges
- *Heal Thyself for Health and Longevity* by Queen Afua
- Africanamericanveganstarterguide.com/
- Peta.org/living/food/african-americans-animal-rights/
- Vegansociety.com
- 22daysnutrition.com
- Purplecarrot.com
- Pcrm.org
- *Follow Your Kind.* Podcast with Krystyna R.
- *The Exam Room.* Podcast by Physicians Committee for Responsible Medicine
- Stic.Man of Dead Prez. *The Workout.* (album) 2011.

Step #11 – Working with Passion

- TrishAhjelRoberts.com/resources for music, meditations and affirmations for passion
- *Thinking Outside the Chrysalis: A Black Woman's Guide to Spreading Her Wings* by Trish Ahjel Roberts
- Research trade organizations, publications, websites and blogs in areas of interest to you.
- Identify Meetup, Facebook and LinkedIn groups in your areas of interest.
- Support national and local charities by volunteering. (Refer to

Step #6—Generosity for some of my favorites.)

🕊 *Self Made: Inspired by the Life of Madam CJ Walker.* Directed by Kasi Lemmons. Starring Octavia Spencer and Tiffany Haddish. Spring Hill Entertainment, 2020.

🕊 *A Ballerina's Tale.* Directed by Nelson George. Starring Misty Copeland. Urban Romances Inc., 2015.

🕊 *The Banker.* Directed by George Nolfi. Starring Anthony Mackie. Apple TV, 2020.

🕊 *Harriet.* Directed by Kasi Lemmons. Starring Cynthia Erivo. Perfect World Pictures, 2019.

🕊 *Ali.* Directed by Michael Mann. Starring Will Smith. Columbia Pictures, 2001.

🕊 *What Color is Your Parachute?* by Richard N. Bolles

Step #12 –Freedom

🕊 TrishAhjelRoberts.com/resources for music, meditations and affirmations for surrender

🕊 *Thinking Outside the Chrysalis: A Black Woman's Guide to Spreading Her Wings* by Trish Ahjel Roberts

🕊 *Live In Wonder: A Journal of Quests, Quotes, & Questions to Jumpstart Your Journey* by Eric Saperston with Mirabella Love

🕊 *Mind-Blowing Happiness™ Guide to Self-Care* (e-book) by Trish Ahjel Roberts available at TrishAhjelRoberts.com/resources.

Music Playlist

1. Erykah Badu. "Bag Lady." *Mama's Gun*, 2000.
2. India Arie. "I Am Light." *Songversation*, 2013.
3. Fire Island featuring Marc Anthoni. "If You Should Need a Friend." *Junior Boy's Own*, vinyl, 1995.
4. Janelle Monáe. "I Like That." *I Like That*, 2018.
5. Bob Marley. "Redemption Song." *Uprising*, 1980.
6. Red Hot Chili Peppers. "Give It Away." *Blood Sugar Sex Magik*, 1991.
7. Sting. "If You Love Somebody Set Them Free." *The Dream of the Blue Turtles*, 1985.
8. Sly and The Family Stone. "Que Sera, Sera" (Whatever Will Be, Will Be)." *Fresh*, 1973.
9. India Arie. "Slow Down" *Voyage to India*, 2002.
10. Marvin Gaye. "Mercy, Mercy Me (The Ecology)." *What's Going On?* 1971.
11. Rihanna. "Work." *Anti,* 2016.
12. Pharrell Williams. "Freedom." (single) 2015.

Made in the USA
Monee, IL
22 October 2021